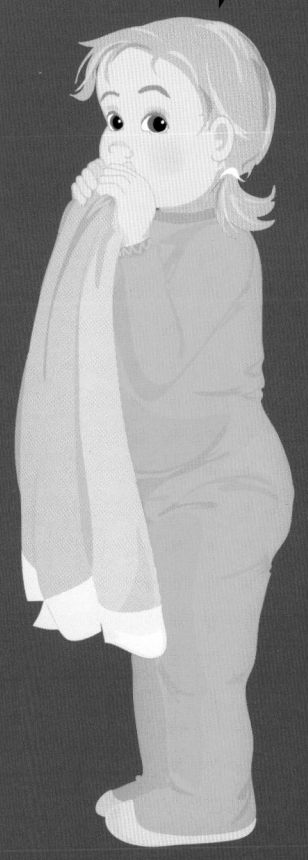

I'm scared.

Babies and toddlers can't say "I'm scared" in words. Instead, they tell you with tears. To comfort little ones who are frightened or upset, try the following ideas.

Little Kids

Talk

Babies may not understand *what* you say, but they react to the *way* you say it. Talk to them in a low, soothing voice, and keep talking even if you run out of things to say. For instance: "There, there, baby, everything's O.K., you're O.K., everyone loves you, you're going to be fine, you'll see, it's O.K."

Walk

Movement helps calm kids. Pick up a baby or toddler and walk her around the room or house.

Touch

Start with a hug. Move on to patting or rubbing the baby's back, bottom, or chest. Find a steady rhythm she likes, and rub or pat firmly (but not hard enough to hurt).

Distract

Once the baby starts to calm down, distract her with a toy, a book, a peek out the window, or anything else that catches her interest.

Use body language

Long before they learn to talk, children communicate with body language. You can use this special language to comfort kids. Kneel beside the child so you can look into her eyes. Smile. Tilt your head to one side. After you do this a few times, it will feel natural. Try it—it works!

Super Sitter Secret

Travel light

"I *always* bring a night-light in my backpack when I go babysitting. Some kids are very afraid of the dark!"

Joan
Rhode Island

Three and Up

Kids this age can usually tell you exactly what's scaring them. That helps! Once you know what's frightening them, you can do something about it. Here are some of the most common fears children have.

The dark

Don't flip off the lights and race to a lit room yourself. This can make kids nervous about the dark. Dim the lights or put on a night-light. Then let them see that you're not afraid. Sit on the bed and tell them a story. Or give them a favorite stuffed animal or doll. Say, "Put your baby to sleep." This puts them in charge of their fear.

Stormy weather

You'll find out about this fear only if a thunderstorm actually happens while you're babysitting. Stay with the child. Turn on a light even if he's already gone to bed. Talk to him about what a thunderstorm really is, in words he can understand: "Thunder is the noise we hear when two big rain clouds bump into each other up in the sky. Isn't that cool?" Hug him, play with him, sing songs, tell funny stories, or do anything else that takes his mind off the storm outside.

Scary thoughts or dreams

Tell the child to imagine that his mind is a television and he's holding the remote control. Have him imagine that he's clicking the remote and changing the channel from a scary show to a silly one. Sit with him until he's asleep.

Your Turn

Night noises

You just finished watching a scary movie on TV, and now you hear strange noises in the house. What do you do when *you're* scared?

The best cure for this kind of fear is prevention. Don't watch scary movies or read scary books—especially while you're babysitting. If you do get nervous, check the house to reassure yourself that everything's secure. Call a parent or a neighbor. If you're truly convinced you hear an intruder, call 911. It's better to be safe than sorry.

Mash the monsters!

No matter how often you reassure them, some kids will still be afraid of things that go bump in the night. If this happens, get creative. Here's what other sitters have done to move the monsters out.

"I bring a spray bottle filled with water. At bedtime, I tell the kids it's monster spray and spray it around the room. Then I tuck it back into my pack, and they feel safe!"

Channing
Kansas

"The four-year-old that I watch is afraid of the dark. So we surround the bed with his stuffed animals. We call them Super Toys. They keep out bogeymen and ghosts."

Laura
Maryland

"If the kids say there's a monster under their bed, I put a carrot into a sack and slip it under the bed. I tell them monsters love carrots, and they shrink to fit inside the bag. After a few minutes I grab the bag and put it into the garbage can. They always fall asleep right after that!"

Kelly
California

The kids you're babysitting insist they always have candy with dinner. You know that's not true—but what do you do?

You're in Charge

Kids can be surprisingly persuasive when they want you to do things their way. Try these wise words the next time you don't know what to say.

Offer a substitute
She says: "My parents make me hot chocolate every night—and they let me drink it in bed."

You say: "Hot chocolate in bed doesn't seem like a good idea to me. I'll give you a glass of milk and read you a story while you drink it in the kitchen."

Offer a substitute that you feel good about. Ask parents about the rules when they get home so that next time you'll know.

Give her a choice
She says: "I just want to jump from the table onto the sofa *one* time."

You say: "You have a choice. You can either climb down from the table yourself, or I can help you down. Which do you choose?"

When you give children a choice, you're teaching them that you make the rules but that they have some control over what happens.

Think about safety

She says: "Don't tell my parents! I'll never ride my bike without my helmet again, I promise!"

You say: "I do have to tell your parents—not to be mean, but because I know they care about you. When it comes to your safety, they have to know exactly what happened."

When the parents return, let them know what the child has done. Remember: Your job is to keep kids safe, even if it makes you unpopular.

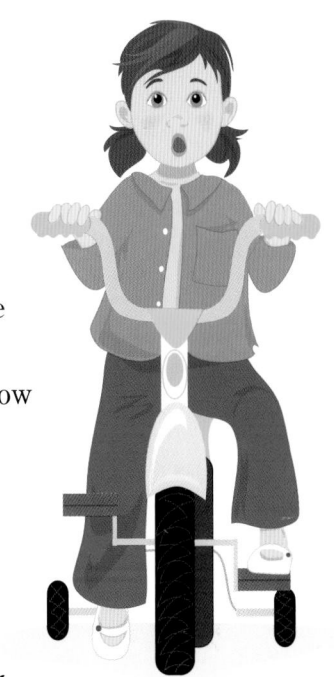

Enforce the rules—calmly

He says: "I won't get ready for bed! I hate you! I wish you would go away and never come back!"

You say (calmly): "I'm sorry you feel that way. But you still have to brush your teeth."

Sometimes kids say mean things to see how you'll react, but they'll usually calm down and do what you ask. If you feel a child really doesn't like you, let his parents know. Say, "I'm sorry, but Henry and I aren't a good fit." They'll understand.

Make an agreement

She says: "I'm not cleaning up my toys, and you can't make me!"

You say: "I can't make you, and I'm not going to try. But if you don't clean up, I won't have time to read you a story because I'll be too busy cleaning up toys. And I will have to tell your parents what happened."

Show the child that his behavior has consequences. And if you do decide to take away a story or a treat, don't back down.

Stay calm

He says: "I'm not going to bed! No, no, no, no, no!"

You say: Nothing. You don't want to keep the tantrum going. Stay near him, but let him cry. He will eventually calm down.

Sometimes silence works best. Kids try tantrums to see if they'll get what they want. If tantrums work, they'll keep throwing them—which is not good for anybody.

Super Sitter Secret

You're the boss

"Even though you may not feel like it, you are in charge. The kids look up to you!"

Heather
Connecticut

Poop.

Never changed a diaper? It's easier than you think. But before you face your first diaper duty, ask an adult to show you how. Then remember these tips.

Get Ready!

Stock supplies

Once the baby's on the table, you don't want to leave her, so get supplies ready *before* you lay her down: baby wipes, clean diapers, and any cream or ointment the parents have asked you to apply. Keep supplies out of the way so the baby can't kick them off. Also, place a garbage can or diaper pail nearby to dispose of used diapers.

Never leave her

If you can, try to keep one hand on the baby so she doesn't fall off the table— and *never* leave her side.

Distract her

Babies love to watch things that move. If there's a mobile over the changing area, blow on it or tap it right before you get to work. You can also talk, sing, or make faces at the baby.

Keep her busy

Give the baby something to hold or chew during a diaper change so that her hands don't get in your way. If no toys are handy, offer a clean diaper or washcloth.

Be gentle

To avoid bumping the baby's head, keep one hand under the back of her head as you lay her down.

Remove her clothes

When removing the baby's pants, keep a hand on her. If her clothes are dirty, put clean ones on after you've changed the diaper.

Poop.

47

Diaper Demo

Once everything's prepared, you're ready to change the diaper.
Follow these step-by-step instructions, and changing a diaper will
be a snap!

1. Undo diaper. Gently
   grasp baby's ankles
   and lift. Slide diaper
   from under baby's
   bottom. Fold edges
   so nothing falls out.

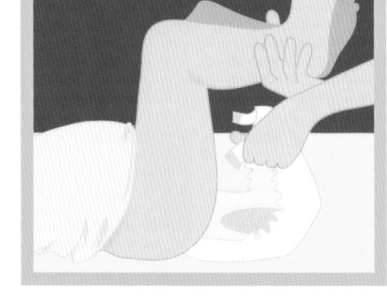

2. Set baby's bottom
   down gently. Dispose
   of used diaper, but
   keep a hand on baby
   at all times. Even a
   newborn can roll off
   a changing table.

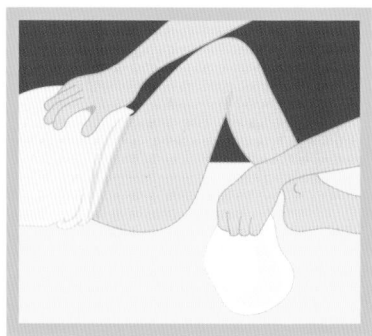

3. Carefully wipe baby's
   bottom from front to
   back with a baby wipe.
   For boys, lay a clean
   diaper over the penis to
   avoid surprising showers.

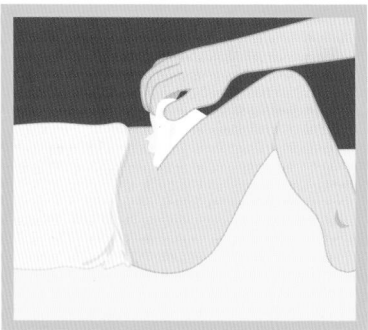

4. Apply lotion if parents
   have asked you to. Then
   gently grasp baby's feet
   and lift. Slide a clean
   diaper under baby's
   bottom and fasten the
   tabs from back to front.

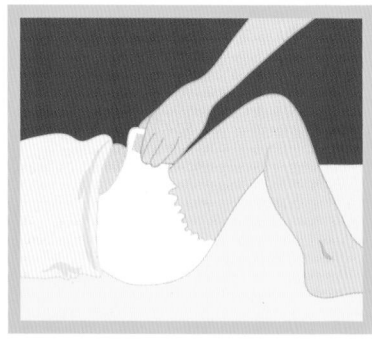

5. Dress the baby in clean clothes. Then set her someplace safe—in a crib or on the carpet where you can see her—while you wash your hands.

Super Sitter Secret

Bathroom break
"If you *have* to go to the bathroom while watching a baby, put her in a crib or a playpen while you're gone. Never leave her out."

Andi
Florida

Poop.

Potty Plan

Most kids begin toilet training between ages two and three. And every child goes through the process differently. To help them do their best, try these tips:

❑ When a child says she has to go potty, she means *right now!* So don't say, "Wait a minute." Stop what you're doing and take her to the bathroom.

❑ Never scold a child who goes to the bathroom in his pants. If he doesn't make it to the toilet, praise him for trying, and help him into clean clothes. When he does go potty on the toilet, always praise him.

❑ Boys may sit down to pee—it's neater that way. If they want to stand, help aim their bodies so they're peeing into the toilet.

❑ Kids under five may need help cleaning up after pooping. Ask them to stand and lean over. This makes your job easier. Remember to wipe front to back.

❑ Two- and three-year-olds often forget to go to the bathroom. Every so often, ask them, "Do you need to go potty?" But don't force the issue.

❑ Make sure the child washes before she leaves the bathroom. Slip soap into her hands and turn on warm water. Remember to wash your hands, too, especially after changing diapers.

Stop accidents before *they happen.*

Safety First

Check for potential hazards

Watch out for possible dangers like matches, electrical cords, plastic bags, cleaners, medicines, tools, and even clutter. Use childproof locks and childproof sockets if they're available, and keep bathroom doors closed.

Make sure the child can't pull anything off a high area onto herself.

Never tell a stranger that you're alone.

Never leave out knives.

Keep rugs flat so kids won't trip over them.

Don't leave the house

As soon as parents leave, lock all doors. If someone knocks on a door, don't open it. Say, "Mr. Smith can't come to the door, but he asked me to take a message." If someone calls, don't tell the caller you're alone. Say, "I'm sorry, Ms. Smith isn't available right now. Can I take a message?"

Know your job site

Ask parents where they keep the first-aid kit, flashlight, and fire extinguisher. Ask how to work the alarm system, the smoke detector, and any equipment you'll be allowed to use, such as the DVD player, TV, or microwave.

Know where the emergency equipment is kept.

Keep plants out of reach.

FIRST AID

Keep all cabinets shut.

Face pot handles toward the back of the stove.

Ow!

Always keep an eye on children

In the blink of an eye, babies can stuff tiny objects into their mouths. Toddlers can slip into pools, tubs, or toilets. Older kids can disappear around a corner. So keep your eyes on kids at all times. Continue to check on them even after they go to bed.

Be Prepared

Emergencies are less scary when you know what to do. Being prepared will help you to stay calm. Take the Babysitter's Training Course offered by the American Red Cross, or Safe Sitter classes held at a hospital in your community.

No matter how minor a child's injury—from a bee sting to a nosebleed—call the parents. That doesn't mean always call parents immediately. In some cases, you'll need to call 911 or the poison control center, or help the child yourself, before you call anyone. Once the child is out of danger, then inform the parents.

When working around blood, *always* wear rubber gloves. First-aid kits should have gloves, but buy a pair and keep them in your babysitter's bag, just in case.

This is not a first-aid book. Nothing replaces hands-on first-aid training. But the following basic tips will help guide you through emergencies.

Insect stings and bites

If you see a stinger, scrape it off with something stiff, like a credit card or playing card. Wash bites and stings with soap and water. Wrap an ice cube in a paper towel and hold it to a sting to reduce swelling.

Cuts and scrapes

Small cuts and scrapes can bleed quite a bit. Use a clean washcloth to press lightly on the injury until the bleeding stops. Then gently wash the cut with soap and water. Apply a Band-Aid—even if you don't think one is needed. It will make the child feel better.

Nosebleeds

Tilt the child's head forward. Pinch the bottom of the nose closed to stop the bleeding. Never tilt the head backward.

Fever

If a child feels warm to the touch, call the parents. In the meantime, encourage the child to rest and offer her water or juice to drink.

Heavy bleeding

For a wound that spurts or gushes, *call 911 immediately.* If someone else is in the area, ask that person to call 911. Then press a clean cloth firmly against the wound and raise it higher than the heart. Keep pressing for at least five minutes. When the bleeding stops, tape the cloth in place and keep the child warm until help arrives.

Super Sitter Secret

Seeing red

"If kids get a small cut, use a red or dark-colored towel so the blood doesn't scare them."

Sarah
Wisconsin

Choking

If a choking child can't talk, cough, or breathe, you must get rid of the obstruction immediately. *Don't take the time to call 911 unless the child passes out.* (If someone else can call 911 for you, ask him or her to do so.) As soon as you've forced the object out, call 911. Choking is *very* scary. Even after you've taken a first-aid course, continue to practice the steps on a doll so you'll be prepared.

For a child:

1. Stand behind the child. Wrap your arms around her waist, as if you're giving her a hug.

2. Make a fist. Place the thumb side against the child's belly, just above the belly button. Grab the fist with your other hand.

3. Thrust or quickly pull your fist up and into the belly. Repeat until whatever the child is choking on pops out of her mouth and she starts to breathe.

4. Call 911 and then the parents.

For an infant:

1. Sit down. Turn the infant onto his belly. Lay him facedown along your arm. Hold his jaw to support his head. Don't cover his nose or mouth. Keep his head lower than his body.

2. Place the heel of your other hand between the shoulder blades. Give five forceful blows with the heel of your hand.

3. While supporting the head, flip the child over onto his back. Place three fingers over his breastbone, between the nipples.

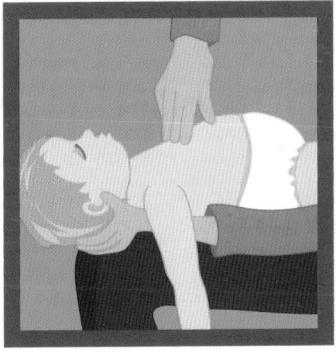

4. Press down firmly on the center of the breast-bone five times. Repeat steps 1–4 until the object comes out.

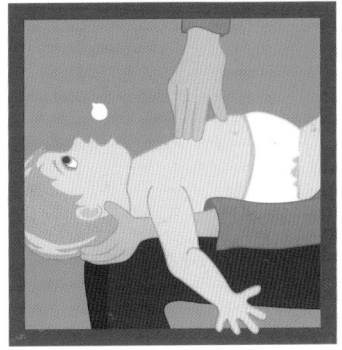

5. Call 911 and then the parents.

Minor burns

Run cool water over red, unbroken skin for at least five minutes. Don't put on a Band-Aid. Don't apply medicine, butter, or any kind of cream. Don't use ice. Small burns are painful, so reassure the child that she'll be O.K. Call the parents. For any burn worse than red skin or a small blister, cool with water and *call 911 immediately*—even if you aren't sure how bad the burn is. Then call the parents.

Swallowing nonfood

If a child swallows anything that isn't food, *call the poison control center immediately* at 1-800-222-1222. (If you can't remember the number, call 911.) Have the bottle nearby when you call. You may be asked to give the child milk or water to drink. Call the parents.

Call 911

If you're faced with any other emergency, *call 911.* The 911 operator may ask for the address and will want to know what kind of emergency is going on. Stay calm, and follow the operator's instructions.

How do you turn a bouncing child into a sleeping angel? Read on!

Make a Timetable

Putting children to bed takes time and planning. Allow 30 to 45 minutes for changing into pajamas, brushing teeth, reading books or telling a story, and cuddling. For instance, if the parents have asked you to put the kids to bed at 8:30, start getting them ready no later than 7:45. Babies and toddlers are a different story. Ask parents what routines they follow to get their tiny ones to sleep.

Note: Babies under age one should always be put to sleep on their backs to reduce the risk of SIDS (Sudden Infant Death Syndrome).

Give plenty of warning

Kids need help moving from one activity to another. Saying, "It's bedtime *right now!*" is sure to cause tears and tantrums. Instead, say, "In ten minutes we're going to get ready for bed."

Follow routines

Kids often have bedtime routines. Ask parents about these. At what time do the kids slip into their pajamas? Do they need to pick up their toys before bed? Can they have a snack? Should you leave the bedroom light on or turn it off?

Share a story

Stories are a great way to end the day. Slip kids into bed, tuck them in, then read or tell them a story. If the kids want to read to you, let them.

Lights-out!

Stick to the routine, especially the first time you sit for a family. When it's time for lights-out, be firm. Kids will know that you mean what you say—and will be much more likely to listen!

Super Sitter Secret

Sweet dreams

"When I'm babysitting a child who can't read, and I read a story at bedtime, I always end with 'and they went to sleep and lived happily ever after,' even though most books don't say that. It helps the child think about going to sleep as a nice thing instead of dreading it."

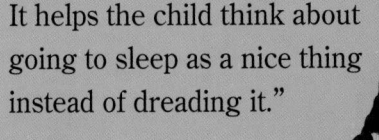

Julia
Delaware

I'm not tired!

Sleepy-time tips

Many children need help falling asleep, especially babies and toddlers. Here are some tried-and-true ways to help.

Rock or carry an infant. Try different moves, such as fast, slow, or up-and-down jiggling, until you find one that works.

Lay a sleeping baby down s-l-o-w-l-y. Dropping him suddenly into the crib will jolt him awake.

Firmly pat or rub the toddler's back or his tummy.* You can try a combination of patting and rubbing. *See the note on p. 60.

Sing to a child once she's in bed. Lullabies are good, but almost any song will help a child settle down.

Put on a night-light. Or turn on a light in the hall or bathroom and adjust the door until it feels right for the child.

Promise to come back and check on the child in 10 or 15 minutes— and make sure you do.

Your Turn

I'm tired!

The kids are asleep, and you're tired, too. Is it O.K. for you to take a nap on the couch?

Falling asleep on the job is unprofessional, and it could be dangerous. Until the parents return, your job is to be alert and in charge. (A good night's sleep the night before should help.) Splash cold water on your face, jog in place—do whatever you must to stay awake.

Here are some other American Girl books you might like:

❏ I read it.
☑ I own it.

❏ I read it.
☑ I own it.

❏ I read it.
☑ I own it.

❏ I read it.
☑ I own it.

❏ I read it.
☑ I own it

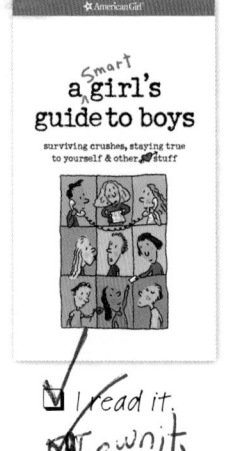

☑ I read it.
☑ I own it